OWT, NOWT & SUMMAT!

A toast to all Tykes

Len Markham

Cartoons by Brian Aldred

COUNTRYSIDE BOOKS
NEWBURY BERKSHIRE

COUNTRYSIDE BOOKS
3 Catherine Road
Newbury, Berkshire

To view our complete range of books,
please visit us at
www.countrysidebooks.co.uk

ISBN 978 1 84674 173 9

To the inimitable Mick Kennedy

Designed by Peter Davies, Nautilus Design
Produced through MRM Associates Ltd., Reading
Printed by Athenaeum Press Ltd., Gateshead

CONTENTS

Foreword 5

Chapter 1 In a Manner o' Speykin' 7

Chapter 2 The Tyke Kitchen.......................................18

Chapter 3 Yorkshire Landmarks....................................28

Chapter 4 Sports and Sporting Heroes.............................37

Chapter 5 Great Moments in History...............................48

Chapter 6 Coal, Wool, Steel and Fish.............................54

Chapter 7 Country Houses...60

Chapter 8 Oddballs and Eccentrics................................66

OWT,
NOWT
& SUMMAT!

FOREWORD

Following on from the success of my book *Ee Up Lad!*, sales of which even permeated the dark Lancastrian badlands to the west of the Pennines, this book seeks a further frolic through the lush garden of Yorkshire dialect, character and history to reveal even more outstanding celebrities, turns of phrase and rib tickling facts and figures. I wallow in the unique oral, cultural, social and sporting traditions that have made Yorkshire one of the most instantly identifiable and smile-provoking counties in England, rampaging through the millennia with a weather-eye cocked for the outlandish and the absurd.

When God made the counties, he made Yorkshire to his own specification and subcontracted the rest. Yorkshire folk have always been aware of this reality and it has imbued in them a restrained and undemonstrative confidence that can be perceived by southern sorts, who have to make do with the minor shires, as arrogance and sullenness.

Sitting on the backbone of England overlooking the largest county in the land, the Tyke looks imperiously out on an area that has more acres than the Bible has words and as many heroes. Yorkshire is bigger than some countries and just as they have developed their own idiosyncrasies and national traits, so has blossomed the inimitable Yorkshire character – the gift of humour, often in situations that would make ordinary mortals weep, setting our race apart.

A Yorkshireman loves his county, such a varied and productive landscape, remote and free from adulteration from its neighbours, breeding rare contentment and an assurance that needs no exaggeration or fancy words. It has also fostered a shamelessly honest bluntness, known universally as 'Yorkshire Bite', such attributes helping to shape the modern world.

In a diaspora begun by religious zealots who sought out the opportunities of North America and by Captain Cook whose sterling voyages aboard the *Endeavour* and *Discovery* opened up Australia and the Pacific regions, the White Rose of Yorkshire has been grafted onto the stock of a hundred nations. Early exports of woollens followed by torrents of manufactured iron and steel goods made the county's international reputation, while pioneering world figures such as William Wilberforce and literary giants like the Brontë sisters did so much to define the character of the dour but ultimately lovable Tyke.

And how would we cope without Yorkshire pudding and an inclination never to use a whole word when a time-and-tongue-saving contraction was available? And where would a confused and disorientated mankind be but for

John Harrison and Percy Shaw, one inventing the marine chronometer that enabled accurate navigation by sea and the other leaving his cat's-eye calling cards on every road on the planet?

From Yorkshire comes the Yorker[1]
Of stealthy balls the chief;
From Yorkshire comes the pudding,
That mates with England's beef;
From Yorkshire comes the cutlery,
That serves the beef to sever;
And other things the Ridings find,
Which makes the county disinclined
To think itself unclever.

So if the towns are boastful,
'Tis not without a cause;
From Whitby with its abbey,
To Ripon with its dawes[2].
But York? Ah, York's the proudest one!
Its pride it hugs and clutches,
And smiling glows because it knows,
It owns the very Yorkist Rose,
The sweetest English Duchess.

With such poetically forceful sentiments, is it any wonder that Yorkshire men and women sometimes appear rather superior? But all is not as it seems. Beneath our seemingly craggy and aloof exteriors ('you can always tell a Yorkshireman, but not much!') and beyond our perceived flinty and down-to-earth speech, we are, when you get to know us, the most companionable, self-deprecating and jolliest people in the world. Traditionally, it is true, we would 'summer and winter you and winter you again' before becoming firm friends. But let us skip the formalities and dive straight in for a feast of friendly fun that I hope will have your collar studs and corset stays popping.

So raise a glass to mirth!

Len Markham

[1] In cricket, a delivery that pitches directly beneath the bat [2] Jackdaws

In a Manner o' Speykin'

Taking my inspiration from Dr Joseph Wright of Bradford who, in the 19th century, was the first systematic compiler of dialect idioms in the country (he founded the Yorkshire Dialect Society in 1901), I have made a lifetime study of the dialect and language of my taciturn and laconic 'see all, hear all, say nowt' Yorkshire friends Bill and Bob, who sit in the snug of the Royal Oak with their pipes and pints watching the world go by.

They will sip and suck for long periods, apparently oblivious to the raging debate about them, until finally they break their silences with a rapier-like wit and wisdom that stuns the throng. Treating words like the precious coins in their pockets - some of these are condemned to a life of hole-wearing - they only exercise their tongues when absolutely necessary, their remarkable word restraint and powers of condensing whole sentences into pithy growls and groans deriving from an absolute and an unquestioning capitulation to the daily oral deluges from their respective spouses, Madge and Gladys.

Once the matriarchs have slipped in their dentures, the pre-breakfast badinage from the bottoms of the stairs in the adjacent Rose and Pine cottages in Bishop Wilton begins slowly and inexorably like this:

Wives:	'Y'up?'
Husbands:	'Ibed.'
Wives:	'Grup?'
Husbands:	'Shrup.'
Wives:	'Grup?'
Husbands:	'Mup.'
Wives:	'Swant?'
Husbands:	'Teggs.'
Wives:	'Becon?'
Husbands:	'Yus.'
Wives:	'T?'

Husbands:	'Yus.'
Wives:	'Uptheer?'
Husbands:	'Yus.'
Wives:	'Theer.'
Husbands:	'Tot! Bloody 'ell! Ah've bunt missen!'

Galvanised by such exchanges into a realisation that the entire English language could be transformed to become much more dynamic and concise – think of the saving in parliamentary time and in the pages of Hansard alone! – I have pioneered in my own household, as a logical progression and formalisation of a process that has been going on in Yorkshire for hundreds of years, the introduction of what I have termed Phonetic Reducibles, or **Ticbulls** for short. Here are some brief examples of the contractions that are frequently heard in the Markham home:

Berpants Babber pants. A **wuzz**, cissy or in the East Riding, a **mammy coddle**. Usually directed at a reluctant child who refuses to jump over the bonfire blindfolded with two fizzing bangers in his back pocket on **Plot Neet**.

Bobadling Bye, bye, darling. Rare parting words substituted for the common **Tirra!** and uttered mincingly with a smile by men on the way to watch Leeds United or Sheffield Wednesday as a prelude to asking, 'Will it be alreet if I joins lads for a swift un after t'game, luv?'

DPM The Louisville Lip gave the world of boxing the 'Ali-Shuffle'; Yorkshire's very own bruiser, former Deputy Prime Minister John Prescott, is countering with the **DPM**, a put-me-down punch line that was the most potent weapon in New Labour's political armoury. Out of the same locker as the **Sleekiss**, the Hull Haymaker as it has become known is particularly effective in curtailing filibustering by members of Her Majesty's Opposition, especially when Mr Speaker has gone for a leak or is tying his shoelaces.

Gnunt Pregnant. 'Why ey, lass, that's good news ... I'll get his name darn fer t'darts team.'

Gremoff This growled utterance encapsulates the romantic spirit of a whole Shakespearean sonnet in one guttural invitation to a lady to disrobe and prepare for lovemaking. The invitation is usually followed by the warning **Bracethisen**, unless the ambience of the moment is disturbed with the interjection **Bugroff.**

Kshun Sophistication. Not a word you hear regularly outside Harrogate. The latter elongated word drifts delicately like a posh belch from an O-shaped mouth as if a Betty's éclair was lodged sideways and is pronounced 'Hah-row-gate' ... 'we don't have mice in Harrowgate, we only have rates'. The benchmarks for sophistication in Yorkshire are (a) eating fish and chips from a plate - I blame it all on Harry Ramsden; (b) buying first class stamps; and (c) using towels after a bath - 'Get thick off lad wi' yer underpants and vest and then yer can lig out in front o'fire.'

Lyza Fertiliser. Climate-change-aware Tykes never throw anything away and all organic material is recycled to the compost bin, including the contents of the Hoover bag, dead bluebottles, ghost turds (check your ceiling corners), nail clippings, granddad's and grandma's beard trimmings, pokings from the plug holes and U-bends in the kitchen and bathroom, scrapings from the treads of boots and shoes (a holding device and scraping implement both in fetching pink, have been specially designed and patented for the female hand by blacksmith Ebenezer Spanzeldroop of Booze in Arkengarthdale to allow the cleaning to be accomplished with one hand whilst the other darns socks), soot, and riding school steamers left in the road. And training one's dog appropriately can save hundreds of tons of CO_2 emissions and scores of plastic bags in a lifetime.

Shire dings Yorkshire puddings. Universally loved, the pudding should be eaten as a first course as a dent to the appetite – 'them that eaats most puddin' gets most meeat.' The powder puff General de Gaulle, who declared that the dish was invented in France, was knocked unconscious in 1954 when his open-topped motorcade was hit with a soufflé thrown by a toddler from Doncaster.

Skeeping The allocation of funds for the weekly housekeeping. 'Can I borra summat from t'pot? T'oss in t'two-thirty's a certinty.'

Sleekiss Barnsley kiss. A head butt; a playful but effective skull-to-skull greeting originated by aboriginal Iron Age Brigante warriors and coyly adopted by ladies in the South Yorkshire town in declining male overtures of a sexual nature.

Supwiu? A curt and surly enquiry as to one's state of health or welfare. Usually met with the retort '**Supwithissen**, it's cheaper.'

Tance Reluctance, like my disinclination to switch off the central heating system unless there is an argh! in the month.

Terbottle Hot water bottle. 'O'course yer can, darlin', just this once. But I'd rather yer saved on t'electric. If yer leaves yer bleedin o' t'radiators 'til we gets ready fer bed, yer can 'ave all t' hot watter yer wants.'

Tiruffpoo Anti-dandruff shampoo. The most organic and green-credentialled Yorkshire version of this product is made from urine. 'I've written out t'labels, Gladys ... would you fill t'bottles?' 'What, from 'ere?'

Tralting Central heating. 'I'll switch it off now, luv... tirra. I'm off t'boozer ... shall I fetch yer coat?'

Tox Beetox. A revolutionary, totally organic and most cost-effective cosmetic treatment devised and patented by me to enhance the appearance of Yorkshire women by removing wrinkles, sags and bloatings. Instantly effective with only minor and short-lasting discomfiture from a multiply-injected natural serum synthesised from Fylingdales Moor heather pollen, beetox comes with a year's supply of royal jelly and an annual invitation to attend the Waggle Dance Ball. Patients who suffer from adverse reactions to buzzing in the ears should seek more traditional treatments.

Umaykissmena Imperious but rash enunciation of a Yorkshire husband giving permission for his spouse to greet him with a labial salutation, most wives responding with the riposte known as the Barnsley kiss (see **Sleekiss**).

Zulloil Wuzzle hole. Simple technology at its most energy-efficient best, predating the tumble drier by almost three centuries. In the washhouse wall (the anonymous hole shown in the picture is just round the corner from

Nora Batty's house in Holmfirth), the drilled wuzzle receives a rod end and wet cloth is hung on the rod and shaken dry, the process having the added advantage of providing ideal training for the Yorkshire Women's Shot Putt Team.

Instructions for deployment of wuzzle stick

1. Take wife's vital measurements from ground to shoulder.
2. Measure distance on outside wall.
3. Using ½-inch bit, drill 3-inch deep hole in wall.
4. Place stick in hole.
5. Drape soggy garment over stick.
6. Escort wife to wuzzle zone.
7. Shout 'start!': wuzzling to continue for 10 minutes per garment.

Note: If wife shows signs of flagging after two hours, shout 'stop!', remove immediately and begin emergency muscle-toning sessions with chest expanders.

Ticbulls will inevitably take time to permeate the upper reaches of the more isolated dales, where some farmers still think there is a war on. One broad Yorkshire chap of my acquaintance from Swaledale – he is a recent convert - visited York last year for the first time in his life. Called to give evidence at the County Court in connection with a drunk and disorderly case, he was invited onto the witness stand by a barrister who spoke with an unintelligible accent. Clearly, there is much to do.

BARRISTER: Is the accused a sober man?

WITNESS: Noa, I heard 'im called a tavern slink.

BARRISTER: Is he a person who consumes more than the recommended daily units of alcohol for a man of his size and stature? Does he habitually incline to a drunken state?

WITNESS: Weel, he does incline after a few pints sure enuf, but he'd hev ti be drooned afore he was drunk. He can bide a vast looad o'drink. In fact, he can eeat like an hoss an' all.

BARRISTER: Have you witnessed him drunk?

WITNESS: Nut mortallious, nor nowt o' that theer! Ah've seen 'im market fresh?

BARRISTER: Can you explain what you mean by that terminology, Sir?

WITNESS: He gets market merry.

BARRISTER: *(pulling on his wig)* Do you mean he becomes intoxicated or paralytic? Does he fall about and become incoherent *(pulling on his wig again and whispering)* like you?

WITNESS: Well, mebbe nut, but there's times when he'd nivver git yam if it wasn't fer yon awd meear of his that knaws t'way ez well ez it diz.

BARRISTER: Are you saying, Sir, that the witness enjoys a drink without his faculties becoming impaired?

WITNESS: If theers owt he likes better than a glass of yal, it's two or even mebbe three.

BARRISTER: *(throwing his wig to the floor)* Why can't you answer in plain English, man? For the last time, does he or does he not get drunk?

WITNESS: There's some folks what's that salivated wi' drink they're nivver fairly sowber. Ah s'u'd saay he's nivver wi'out yon. In fact, ti put it in plain English as yer say, he's killin' hissen wi' what he likes an' neea be-God nonsense aboot it. Now mi' lad, why the blazes dint yer ask me that in t'fust place?

THE
BEEROMETER
TO BE HUNG IN A "DRY" PLACE
NOSE WHITE
NOSE PINK
NOSE RED
NOSE PURPLE
NOSE BLUE
NOSE BLACK
NOSE EXPLODES
TEETOTAL
JUST HAD ONE
ONE OVER THE EIGHT
DRUNK
BLIND
PARALYTIC
TIME TO SIGN PLEDGE

I HAD A PROBLEM WITH THEM NIAGARA TABLETS BILL
WHAT, DID THEY MAKE YER PEE?
NO, DAFT BUGGER, THEY'RE FER T'OTHER BUSINESS...REMEMBER?
OH, I DOES BOB. SAY NER MORE. WHAT 'APPENED?

WELL WHEN TIME CUMS WE'D BOTH FORGOTTEN WHY I TOOK BLOODY THINGS IN FIRST PLACE
WHAT DID YER DO?
SHE POTS A COLD COMPRESS ON YON AND RINGS FER T'AMBULANCE

When folks have difficulty in understanding proper Yorkshire, it can lead to terrible confusion, as a transcript of this recent telephone conversation in Batley police station shows. The first policeman was newly recruited from London – bless him!

CITIZEN: There's a F8. Come quick.
FIRST POLICEMAN: Calm down, madam. Speak slowly and tell me what the problem is.
CITIZEN: It's mayhem in 'ere. F8!
FIRST POLICEMAN: Sorry, madam. I'm new here. What's an F8?
CITIZEN: F8, silly bugger! Someone's gunner deea.
FIRST POLICEMAN: (*cupping the telephone and turning apologetically to his colleagues*) I've got a frantic woman on the line who's screaming something about an F8. Is it a peculiar Yorkshire code like 10.4 or something?
SECOND POLICEMAN: Give it 'ere. Hello, luv? I've got yer. There's a fight in the *Black Lion* again. *(loud guffaws)* We'll send a car straight round.

━━━━━━━━━━━━━━━━━━ • TEACH THISSEN TYKE • ━━━━━━━━━━━━━━━━

VOCABULARY

Netty An outside non-flushing toilet. Netties are making a post-credit-crunch comeback in parts of Wakefield, saving households thousands of pounds in water and sewage rates and cutting the fertiliser bills for rhubarb growers.

Alerted to the unique oral traditions of the area, ethnologists from Cambridge University recently arranged to have dinner with a large local farming family. Completely cut off from civilisation by encircling motorways, the farm preserves a cultured language, the professors arriving by helicopter with recording equipment.

'Now think on,' lectures mother as the rotor blades stop and the Yorkshire puddings come out of the oven. 'Speak proper, don't be fratchin' and givin' onny o' yer backslaver. An' frame yersen at table and don't get druffen or ahl clout thee.'

As the beef is carved, the youngest of the five boys fidgets and gets to his feet saying: 'Gie us a lollock o' lean and a lollock o' fat, ma, while I gans down t'netty fer a slash.'

Flushed and embarrassed, mother unleashes a **DPM** and says: 'Ahm sluffened and reet sorry. He's as much manners as mi arse.'

Roar To weep uncontrollably and extremely volubly. The day after a Grassington funeral, the vicar paid a visit to a grieving husband, comforting the man with kind words. 'It's noo gud, vicar,' says he, wringing out his handkerchief. 'T'old stiff 'un were all I 'ad in t'world. Ah've bin roarin' all neet an' all mornin' and efter hez 'ad mi dinner and a nice sup o' yal, Ah'm gunner roar a lot moor.'

The Tyke Kitchen

Before we start, we will say the Yorkshire Grace Before Meals:

Lord bless us all, and mek us able,
To clear all t'food that's on t'table.

Now, negatively, but with no apology, we begin in the present-day Tyke kitchen, with a salutary lesson graphically demonstrating what gender imbalances have been wrought in the workplace by generations of totally biased sexual equality legislation. The male victim here shown (his name is withheld and his face has been electronically distorted – as if it needed to be – to protect his identity) shows early signs of Irritable Bowl Syndrome.

How times change! But now that we have got that off our chests, we move back in time, forgetting about microwave contraptions, ready-made meals, fancy-Dan food and foul-mouthed celebrity chefs (remembering the old Yorkshire proverb 'God sends the meat but the Devil sends the cooks'). We can reminisce about the olden days when plain, honest-to-goodness food was the norm, when women knew their place and young chaps waxed lyrical about the ideal wife:

I want a lass, I want a lass,
That knows when muck wants shiftin',
She must wash a sheet as white as snow,
And do her work while singin';
She must hold a plough, scrub, mangle, sow,
And keep a swipple swingin'.

The paramount requirement of such a lass, of course, was the ability to cook a Yorkshire pudding. So important was this skill that in some country parishes, local vicars and priests spoke about it in their sermons, urging

*She uses ivvery flamin' pot in t'place. Willie Wilberforce
wud ton in 'is grave.*

parishioners during the proclamation of wedding banns to report any culinary impediments that might jeopardise the tying of the knot. Away from the church, along with minor homilies about the birds and the bees, mothers strenuously briefed the betrothed on the alchemy of making batter, passing on the scribbled recipe along with other family treasures, like grandmother's golden ring and her best china.

'Oh! Forget about that! Can she mek a proper Yorkshire puddin'?'

It is the case, as with anything precious, that counterfeits abound and we all have experienced the utter disappointment of ordering Yorkshire pudding in some highbrow restaurant or pub, only to see a perspiring waiter wobbling in holding a flaccid and tasteless impostor that has been in the making two days, the table groaning under the weight of a confection that is more suitable to plugging breaches in dams than eating.

In charity to your host, you take a deep breath and chuckle insanely, taking up your fork to prod the beast as if it were some stranded walrus on Filey sands. The implement quivers in the blubber, rebounds and hits you in the eye and you sob, asking for forgiveness and a glass of fruit juice. If you served an abomination like this in my great-grandmother's farmhouse kitchen she would have flayed you alive.

Here is how she made puddings in her Yorkshire range, as her lovely old rhyme shows:

Real Yorkshire Puddin'

Real Yorkshire puddin' is a poem in a batter,
It melts in yer gob just like snow.
Now harken to this and don't int'rupt,
Skimmed milk? No! No! No!

Tek a pint o' moo's glory and mix it wi' flour,
A smidgen o' watter run cowld,
Add two farmhoose eggs an' stir it aboot,
'Til creamy, t'bubbles enfold.

Half-hour it stands and it's ready fer t'tins,
Beef fat to be spittin' real hot,
Pour in wi' a siz, ten minutes it is,
An' serve wi' a foamin' great pot!

She was fond of a jug of homebrew, was great-grandmother and could sup me under the table!

Such plain food, cooked to perfection by a homegrown lass, was the epitome of Yorkshire cooking. Folk in the county like their grub in ample portions, and although it is often alleged that a Yorkshireman will defer expenditure on clothing and will cut a currant in two with the utmost secrecy, he will not spare expense where eating is concerned. The old adage: 'Back will trust but belly won't' sums the matter up precisely. Infants have equally healthy appetites and are known in Yorkshire as 'bread snappers' or 'gob slotchs' with good reason, the feeder demonstrating some caution by keeping the bowl at arms length.

So, apart from the inimitable Yorkshire pudding, what other comestibles is the county famous for? Why, its beer (Yorkshire Stingo), Wensleydale cheese, rhubarb (over 90% of the rhubarb grown in the British Isles comes from Yorkshire), Harrogate toffee and ginger biscuits, and its bacon and ham of course!

A pocket full o'money an' a cellar full o'beer,
A good fat pig that'll last ya all t'year.

Every cottage plot once had its pigsty and the labouring man would rather invest in old Snorkel than put money in the bank. He would cosset the swine, feeding it kitchen waste and leftovers, the dregs from great-grandmother's brewing operations imparting a terrific flavour when 't'time came'. Neighbours galore attended the ritual despatching. Bacon and hams, sausages, spare ribs, lard by the jar full, black pudding and a boiled head for the dogs, all were rendered in just a few hours.

The bacon and hams were salted and smoked, using old timber from York Minster if it was available and, holy of holies, the pork pies would appear steaming from the oven, making grown men like Sam Postlethwat from Bingley shake and drool all down their fronts in anticipation:

'I gets me gob round rim and sucks pastry fust, teking it slow like. Yer should never rush either a bit o' back'ards and for'ards or eatin' a pork pie. Then I twiddles me tongue and meks an 'oil in t'crust, stickin' it in and feeling fer t'meaat, letting t'hot, sweet juices run down me chin and baptise me tonsils. Finally, as if I were wi' our lass at t'back o' fish 'oil on a Satda neet, I get's me nashers round t'lumps and consummates job, burrowin' me whole faace in it as me body quivers wi' ecstasy.'

Some Yorkshire specialties like pork pie and fish and chips served with mushy peas act on the palate like a sensual taser. One of my favourite Yorkshire puddings using forced rhubarb is electrifying, especially when served with a bottle of my favourite Yorkshire beer.

He: 'Will yer show us yer nuts?'
She: 'Onny if yer shows me yours.'

'I twiddles me tongue and meks an 'oil in t'crust...'

Rhubarb Hot Cake

Mixture

8 oz raising flour
Quarter teaspoon grated nutmeg
1 egg
1 oz butter
¼ pint milk
Pinch salt

Filling

½ lb rhubarb
2 oz sugar
½ oz butter

Method

Sieve the flour and salt and rub in the butter to form fine breadcrumbs.
Add sugar. Mix in the milk and egg to form soft dough. Halve the mixture
and roll both halves out to 7-inch diameter rounds. Place first round on a
baking sheet and sprinkle with chopped rhubarb and sugar and dot with the
butter. Divide second round into strips with a knife and lay over the filling.
Bake in a moderately hot oven at 375°F (gas mark 5) for 40 minutes. Dust
with icing sugar and serve hot with cream, extra stewed rhubarb and a glass
of Old Peculier.

And now we will say the Yorkshire Grace After Meals:

We thank thee, Lord, for what we've getten,
But if there'd been more we could have etten,
And yet we'll not scoff nor scorn,
But pray that there'll be more by morn.

● TEACH THISSEN TYKE ●

VOCABULARY

Kecks Trousers. 7ft 3in failed jockey Jeremiah Sidebottom from Bingley was so bow-legged that a rainbow formed when he passed water, and the poor man was unable to buy off-the-peg trousers anywhere. But bespoke tailor Manny Cohen from Leeds came to the rescue.

'My life! Mr Sidebottom,' said Manny, straining and curving his tape to take the inside leg measurement. 'And which side do you hang?'

'Oh, t'buggers never hangs, Manny lad. Yer'l 'ave ti' pleat 'em a bit.'

Sluffened Upset or put out. 'Ah's sluffened ti' say Ah's deean onny tahm na,' shouted 93-year-old Eli Grimley from his sick bed. 'Ah's nobbut walking aboot ti' save fewnril expenses.'

'But tha's still i'bed, fatha,' responded daughter Hilda from the foot of the stairs.

'Ah is, Hilda lass, but up ti' a few months sen Ah alus got up bi fower o'clock in t'mornin' an' cud eaat a lump o' cowld fat bacon ti me breekus. Na Ah can lie quite contented till five o'clock an' Ah can't leeak at fat bacon. Ah can eaat nowt but two or three eggs ti my breekus so Ah kna it's ower wi' ma – Ah's deean.'

'Well git on wi' it, fatha, Ah's got puddin's ter mek.'

'An' will there be apple pie and drop o' summat ti' keep cowld art, ar Hilda? Ah's a bit peckish.'

'NOTICE TO BUTCHERS – MEAT MUST BE WELL HUNG'

Yorkshire Landmarks

A landmark is any geographical or man-made object that you can orientate by when the old internal navigation system has been degraded by a surfeit of alcoholic beverage ('he's kalied') or when one is recovering from cranial damage inflicted by a virago wielding a blunt instrument ('missis brayed him wi' a rollin' pin').

To make the point, I show here a typical street sign in Chiserley near Mytholmroyd, erected to remind inebriated or star-seeing mill workers to stop climbing. What would offcumdens make on it?

And what do the myriads of tourists in York think of this? 'I'm proper flummoxed.'

And tell me what more suitable location could be found for a 'reet good fratchin' session' than this spot in Whitby?

Next up is the picture of a plaque seen on a house in Snaith. Is this the epitome of Yorkshire non-pretension?

Our illustrated tour of the county taking in those unusual landmarks that the common guidebooks leave out, leads us to Huddersfield where generations of locals have stared jealously at the imposing figure of a lion perched high on a plinth atop the Lion Chambers in St Georges Square. Some while ago, old Lenny threatened public safety, building control inspectors needing more than a fig leaf and super glue to prevent a tragedy.

Old Lenny (The threat of immediate emasculation caused the beast to whimper uncontrollably.)

'Nay lad... Ah'll 'ave ti pass on t'snooker toneet ... summat else 'as cum up.'

Now, unusually, we move indoors as any piece of furniture that becomes famous as the biggest in the world deserves its mention in this pantheon of Yorkshire landmarks. Pictured is the largest bed ever made, constructed under Henry VIII's royal warrant by Yorkshire sleep specialist Horace Ontil of the Land of Nod near Holme on Spalding Moor in 1536, its specification demanding more timber than the *Mary Rose* and more recoil from its giant mattress than that from the entire ship's cannon.

The bed is seen here undergoing client assessment and spring trials. The bed's impact-damaged legs were eventually replaced and it was converted to become a two-bedroom mobile home for a troupe of acrobatic dwarfs with the Moscow State Circus in 1982.

Into the wild Yorkshire countryside now, we stop short of a boiling torrent that is the ultimate challenge for dare devils or duffers as they are known in these parts. The Strid near Bolton Abbey is a constriction of the River Wharfe that runs fast and deep. 'Last man ti jump buys t'ale,' is a common cry of the barmpot who usually ends up 50 miles downstream in Tadcaster, stuck in the outlet pipe of John Smiths Brewery and providing a banquet for pike.

*'Colours reet enough and it's gotten a fine 'ead on it, granted ...
but I'd be peeing all neet.'*

'I came, I saw, I gave the Yorkshire buggers a reet good hidin.'

Back in the city we doff caps to our conqueror, the Roman Emperor Constantine who is seen here outside York Minster flashing his knees and twiddling a giant toothpick. Over his left shoulder is the fabled Sack of Rome (in case it comes on to rain) presented to him by cohorts of the Ninth Victrix Legion after they had completed the annual ceremonial delivery of free coal to the plebeians in Parliament Street.

'Prepare ye the haggis, Fiona. I'll clout the warder when he comes in.'

Into the Dales, we fetch up at Bolton Castle, where Mary Queen of Scots was incarcerated in a suite of rooms at the top of the tower at Elizabeth I's pleasure. Denied anything that could be used as a weapon and locked in every night with only a vat of Johnny Walker and a very large bucket for company, here we see her with two of her ladies-in-waiting plotting her infamous escape to Leyburn.

Ranging the county, we arrive in the land of the Loiners in Leeds, taking a peep trackside of cheeky traffic on the Middleton Railway, the oldest in the world, founded in 1755 as a wooden horse-drawn waggon-way. All steamed up at the price of horse and fodder prices at the time of the Napoleonic wars, local engineers John Blenkinsop and John Murray decided to mechanise and by 1812 washer women lineside were waving their besoms and complaining about soot on their smalls.

To finish this whistle-stop tour of Yorkshire, we arrive in the town of Halifax. Take a gander round the borough's mill and clothing shops if you must but remember to keep your head, and I do insist that your hands remain in your pockets, as I am not sure whether the ancient byelaw that dealt with miscreants who stole 'cloth or any other commodity of the value of thirteen pence half-penny' has been repealed. Repeat this extract from the 18-line Thieves Litany to make sure you keep your next appointment with your barber and visit the site of the old gibbet whose use preceded that of the French guillotine by several centuries.

At Halifax, the law so sharp doth deal,
That who so more than 13 pence doth steal;
They have a blade most wondrous quick, and well,
Sends thieves all headless unto Heaven or Hell.

'Ah! tell t'Fat Controller yer driving wi' no hands.' 'Anymore backslaver from you, Tom, an' ah! pee in yer firebox.'

TEACH THISSEN TYKE

VOCABULARY

Bray Therapeutic chastisement. Before flying off to begin filming *The Sound of Music*, actress Julie Andrews was enrolled on a governess-training course in Bowes, North Yorkshire. Educational psychologist and slap, bang and wallop specialist Wackford Squeers V, the principal of the Dotheboys Hall Academy, instructed Miss Andrews on the finer points of child management, stressing the need for discipline and the regular deployment of the cane.

'Yer must gi'e the young uns a reet good brayin' every day, Julie, whether they needs it or not. If they cums to tha freetened sayin' Ah've bin bitten on t'arse bi a dog, a bee's stung mi on t'lug or Ah'm reet browned off, yer must gie 'em summat ti remember. Wallop 'em. Tha'll thank yer forit in t'end. An' think on. That captin fella is as randy as t'lodgin' house cat. He's seven kids already, tha knaws. But no ti' worry, lass. If tha finds thissen up t'spout wi' a bun in t'oven, yer knaws where to cum!'

Kalied Intoxicated. Having consumed prodigious quantities of ale, Jonah and Elsie Watmough from Settle were returning from a christening party early one morning when they decided to take a shortcut across a field. Jonah's cap blew off and he tried on ten crusty cowpats before he found one to fit. When they got home Elsie exclaimed: 'Yer must be kalied, our Jonah! That's not yer cap. It's a mushroom, silly divil! Git fire lit and we'll 'ave us breekus.'

Sports and Sporting Heroes

If sport is any leisure activity played between gentlemen for the purpose of relaxation and amusement, nobody told Yorkshire county cricketer 'Fiery Fred' Trueman or Leeds United's Norman 'Bite Yer Legs' Hunter. One caused cranial star-bursts at every crease in the country, the other made trademark bone-crunching tackles that helped earn his club the epithet 'Dirty Leeds'. But compared to a host of girder-ribbed Yorkshire rugby league forwards who fling more bodies to earth than Genghis Khan's spring offensive, Trueman and Hunter were wimps!

Sport in Yorkshire is a tooth and fang affair, the inculcated passion for competition and winning at all costs even infiltrating the crèche, youngsters of my own era sometimes drawing blood over a game of tiddlywinks. Some of my more sophisticated companions moved on to play conkers but having only bombsites in our neck of the woods, we used house bricks instead, matriculating to more dangerous sports like rushing out and placing pennies on the line in front of the 17.57 from Kings Cross or (and this earned you extra bonus duffing points) riding your bike on the parapet of the bridge as the same express passed under, always remembering to close your eyes to keep out the smoke and grit at the critical moment. We also enjoyed Olympic sailing on the River Aire in Leeds, using a yacht made from lashed-together oil drums with a clothes prop for a mast and a cotton sheet (pinched from the same washing line) for a sail.

And then we had bogey racing. This had nothing to do with competitive little boys attempting to impel nasal pokings down a slide. Bogeys were prototype go-carts manufactured from old floor boarding and pram wheels. Posh, near-on effeminate, lads had a piece of carpet nailed to the driving seat. Aping the exploits of Stirling Moss in a top gear descent of Sutton Bank, we would career down a hill, only the burning rubber on our Jerry Lee Lewis brothel creepers serving as brakes to prevent us sliding under the local grocery delivery van.

'What do us lads need wi' int'national caps when wi got these?'

And then, when we were old enough, we would start to play cricket, football and rugby on the ash-surfaced recreation ground using solid rubber cricket balls, home-made bats, wickets and leather footballs - the ones that absorbed copious amounts of water and collected grit in the lace holes to leave your knees and forehead scratched and bleeding.

Eventually, we saved up our pocket money and visited the grounds of our heroes, watching Brian Close and the young Geoffrey Boycott at Headingley, the marvellous Welsh wizard John Charles newly signed for Leeds United at Elland Road, and rugby league legend Lewis Jones again at Headingley.

But despite Yorkshire playing a pivotal role in the development of popular sport for the masses (Yorkshire won the first rugby league county championship in 1889, repeating the feat six times in the next seven years, only loosing to – spit! – Lancashire), the county has also been noted for less well-known sports like knurr and spell, match fishing, fell racing, pot holing and coal carrying.

'How will they run between t'wickets?'
'No need ti run... we'll knock all sixes.'
'An' t'club'll save loads o' money on boxes.'

If you thought golf was a game of skill, try the infinitely more challenging knurr and spell. Pick up a pommel (the original willow club with a small block of wood at the impact end) and play the prototype royal and ancient game, hitting a knurr (a 1-inch diameter ball made from boxwood or baked clay) that erupts from a spring-operated spell at the speed of light!

Developed in the north of England and dating from at least the 14th century, knurr and spell was a particular favourite of miners and textile workers in the West Riding who made their own equipment. Demanding a large flight area, the game was usually played on waste ground, fields or on adjacent moorland, with the contestants, or laikers as they were known, aiming to hit the ejected knurr as far as possible with the swung pommel.

A popular entertainment, the game was enjoyed by big crowds during the Easter holidays, spectators placing large bets and the participants

WHAT WELL-KNOWN YORKSHIRE PHRASE DOES THAT REMIND YER O' BOB?
ARSE WITHOUT FACE!

competing for cash prizes. At Stainland near Halifax a copper kettle was awarded to the winner. On 6 May 1871, 6,000 spectators congregated at the Belle Vue Ground in Halifax to see the match between champion John Jackson and H. Cockroft of Ovenden. And on 11 November 1889, another Yorkshireman – Fred Moore of Halifax - achieved everlasting fame when he drove a knurr a world record distance of 372 yards, 1 foot and 8 inches at Lightcliffe. Beat that, Tiger Woods!

When knurr and spell lost its popularity, Yorkshiremen had to find a use for all those redundant willow pommels and they naturally turned to match fishing, the first organised competitions in the Victorian period employing primitive rods and reels, catgut and worms. Offering working men a respite from the drudgery and foul air of the coal face, the mill and the blast furnace, match fishing was usually arranged on Sundays, and by the 1950s there was an abandonment of materials like willow, bamboo and the introduction of high-tech glass fibre rods, fixed spool reels and nylon monofilament lines.

Taking themselves to rendezvous points supervising the shipment of massive fishing boxes and rod bags, there would be a mass exodus of working men from the tear-filled embraces of their wives in Leeds, Wakefield, Huddersfield, Sheffield, Hull and Middlesbrough, the anglers congregating on street corners with their spousal hod-carriers to await the arrival of buses. Once on board, as the waving hands disappeared in the distance, the supplies of bottled Tetley's would be broached to huzzahs and, despite the delicacy of the hour, serious boozing would begin accompanied by card playing.

Before the bus reached the environs of the river, a homing device would lock on to the coordinates of the *Anglers Rest*, the men disgorging into the snug bar where the buxom ladies of the village would serve hot and dripping bacon sandwiches washed down with more beer. And then, under the gaze of the largest ever trout to be pulled from the River Nidd before it became polluted with run-off from the sewage works, the draw for pegs would be made, the anglers removing numbered slips from the Hon. Sec's flat cap, some lads taking one look at the numbers and deciding to stay in the pub the whole day.

On the verge of hypothermia, with raindrops slowly infiltrating their socks and underpants, most of the men would spend the next six hours in monastic silence staring at their floats in unblinking concentration

'T'old trout behind t'bar 'll pull yer pint. An' tell 'er a gallon over 'ere in t'aquarium!'

in case they missed the only bite of the day. Rigorous toe wiggling and finger exercises in a bag of seething maggots, afforded some warmth and countered the inclination to rigor mortis. After glumly waving away the weighing scale at the end of the match, the anglers would finally plod back to the warmth of the Royal Oak for a consolation drink before journeying home, where the fishing widow would knowingly inquire: 'Owt?', as she dropped a fillet of cod into the pan.

Tykes who demanded a detectable blood flow in their sport could go the whole hog and take up fell running, the conquest of the highest mountain in Yorkshire, Mickle Fell at 2,591 ft, really getting the heart pumping. It is erroneous to suggest that exponents of Yorkshire fell running actually carried hogs under their arms whilst ascending, although one persistent

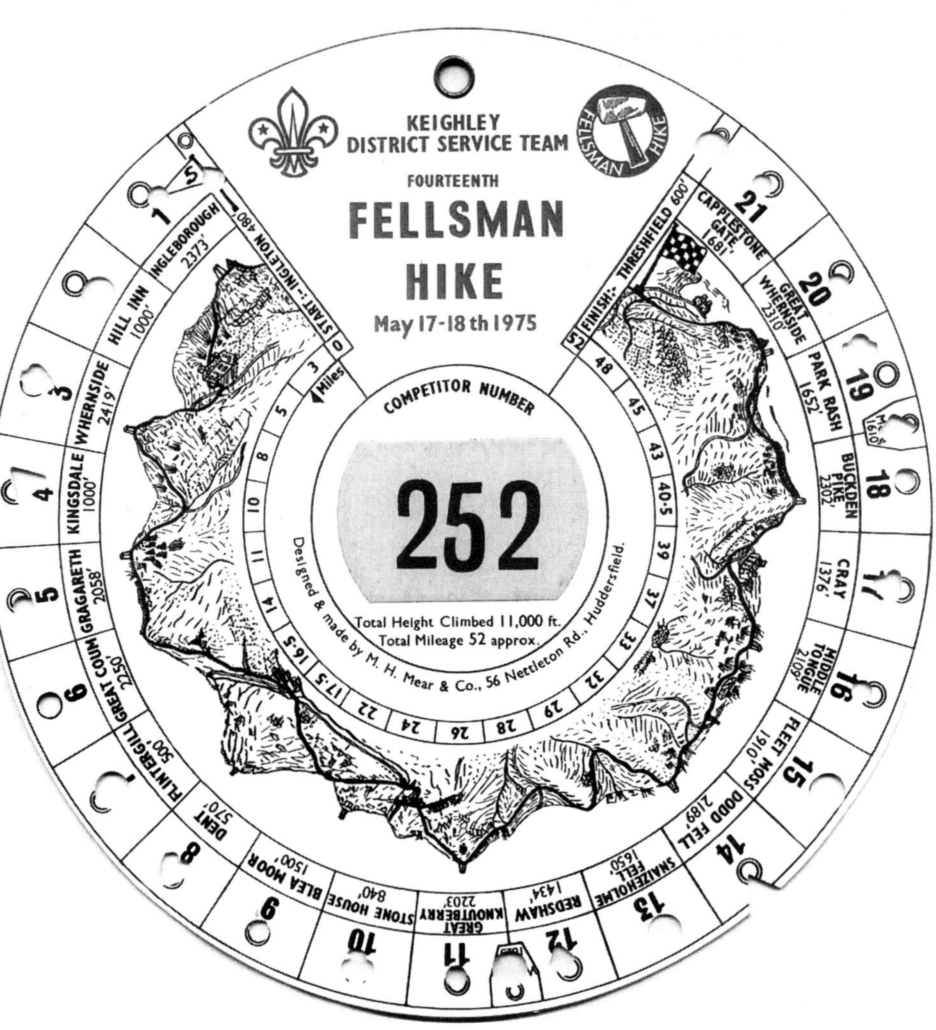

'I wrote my last will and testament on the reverse of my tally disc in the middle of the morass known as Fleet Moss. It washed off.'

winner of the Three Peaks Race – a 22 mile slog between the summits of Penyghent (2,273 ft), Whernside (2,310 ft) and Ingleborough (2,373 ft) – is reputed to have taken a sheep on his training runs. The only thing that I carried on my one near-fatal outing as a competitor in the 52-mile-long 1975 Fellsman Hike (the winner actually ran it in 12 hours!) was a heartfelt wish to live.

Fleet Moss is in the middle of Yorkshire's spectacular limestone wilderness, sportsmen above and below ground finding lots to test the sinews. But before we go on, please read the next paragraph and cut it out to either chew or burn, as we do not want our Gallic friends to become conceited.

In 1882, after two unsuccessful attempts by Englishmen, a Frenchman by the name of Edouard Alfred Martel made the first descent of Gaping Gill – Britain's deepest pothole at 340 ft – and, sacre bleu, he made it on Yorkshire Day, 1 August! Descending into a space that would gobble up St Paul's Cathedral, Martel took 23 minutes to reach the bottom where he made the following notes: '...there is the feeble light of day which, filtering through the spray, with millions of prisms formed by the drops, does not seem like anything upon which human eye has gazed. It affords one the impressive attraction of something never seen before. It is one of the most extraordinary spectacles it has been my pleasure to witness.'

The sport of potholing took off after the first descent of Gaping Gill, human moles with candles on their heads slithering along flooded, cervix-wide passageways, gasping for breath at a little under 0.18 miles per hour, boldly going where no man had shone before. Now, with more sophisticated equipment including torches, aqualungs and self-heating pot noodles, hundreds of speleologists descend on Clapham and district each year to explore Alum Pot, the Kingsdale Master System and the Lancaster Pot and the Easegill Caverns System which, with over 70 known passages, is regarded as the longest and most complex in Britain.

Potholing has had only one known spectator in its history, Patience Outhwaite from Giggleswick having a fetish for ogling virile young men in rubber suits as they penetrated the darkest and hairiest orifices. Enjoying a mass squeeze into Elm Pot in 1973, Patience continued to wait for the emergence until she died of boredom and starvation two weeks later, the speleologists having exited via a connecting tunnel 10 days earlier.

Anyone who chooses to spend time underground in pitch darkness is a lunatic. Would you risk your skull being wedged fast until the next Ice

Age? But if you think potholing is for barmpots, what will you make of coil humping?

It all started innocuously enough in Gawthorpe near Ossett one quiet day in 1963. In the bar of a local pub called the Beehive Inn, local coal merchant Amos Clapham was enjoying a drink with his friend Reggie Sedgewick when in breezed Lewis Hartley. Intruding on the conversation, the newcomer slapped Reggie on the back and shouted: 'Ba gum, lad, tha' looks buggered!'

Affronted, a startled Reggie rejoined: 'Ah'm as fit as thee, an' if tha' dun't believe me gerra bagga coil on thi' back an' Ah'll get one on mine, an Ah'll race thee to t'top o' t'wood!'

While Hartley was ruminating on his challenge, Secretary of the Maypole Committee Fred Hirst had a brainwave, cautioning: 'Owd on a minute: am't we bin lookin' fer summat ter do on Easter Munda? If we're gonna 'ave a race let's 'ave it then. Let's 'ave a coil race!'

And so began the unique *Guinness Book of Records*-entered World Coal Carrying Championships for both men and women.

The events are held every Easter Monday over an 1108.25 yd course starting at the Royal Oak pub in Gawthorpe and ending at the maypole on the village green. The current records stand at 4 minutes 6 seconds for the men and 5 minutes 5 seconds for the ladies. Contestants have to carry 1 cwt sacks of coal (25 lbs for the ladies), the first humpers to drop their loads at the foot of the maypole being declared the winners. Non-Yorkshire passport holders are not barred from the event and even an American has taken part.

Interestingly, brawn does not seem to confer an advantage. The ideal competitor weight is around 10½ stones. Contestants prepare hard for the big day, one former winner, a farmer, revealing that he trained by running uphill with a 'seek o' spuds on mi' back'.

The event is the only sport that is unique to Yorkshire ... and so to a challenge that might get the eyes of the Maypole Committee popping. I can think of only one other county in England that contests a world championship sporting event solely within its boundaries. I throw down the gauntlet to Suffolk's world champion Blyth Valley Dwile Flonkers, to come to Yorkshire, take us on and 'get a bagga coil on thi' backs' if we respond by visiting Suffolk and making a bid for world supremacy.

Just to get my compatriots in the mood at the Royal Oak, dwile flonking is ritualised and competitive beer swilling, teams consisting of eight men, a circle enclosing a member of the opposing team – the flonker - who flings an ale-soaked dwile in their direction. Direct hits require each man to drain a chamber pot full of ale. I am sending invitations and copies of this book to the Secretaries of the Gawthorpe Maypole Committee and the Blyth Valley Dwile Flonkers hoping that both challenges can be taken up ... but not on the same day.

TEACH THISSEN TYKE

FOLK RHYMES

Under water men shall walk,
Shall ride, shall sleep, shall talk.
In the air men shall be seen
In white, in black and green.

(Old Mother Shipton's prophesy)

Down in the deep the stool descends,
But here, at first, we miss our ends;
She mounts again and rages more,
Than ever vixen did before.
If so my friend, pray let her take,
A second turn into the lake;
And rather than your patience lose,
Thrice and again repeat the dose.
No brawling wives, nor furious wenches,
No fire so hot but water quenches.

(An ode to a very effective cure for gossiping women)

This yah neet, this yah neet,
Ivvery neet an' all,
Fire an' fleet an' cannule leet,*
An' Christ tak up thy saul.

(The first of nine other verses of the 'Lyke Wake Dirge' formerly recited at Cleveland funerals. Adopted as the anthem of walkers who complete the arduous 42-mile hike from Osmotherley to Robin Hood's Bay.)
*water

Great Moments in History

Yorkshire has been steeped in history since the Great Flood and it was particularly damp at the end of the last Ice Age. Once the waters receded, the county developed as a Garden of Eden, the repealing of all EC Common Agricultural Policy regulations about forbidden fruit attracting successive eager waves of Celts, Anglo-Saxons, Romans and Danes. Their conquests, rapes and pillages, religious reforms, industry, art and massive talent for drinking fine ale made Yorkshire the place it is today.

But was the creation of the greatest county in England circumstance, happenstance, or boozy pure chance?

After Harold's victory at the Battle of Stamford Bridge in 1066, what would have happened six weeks later at Hastings if the old boy had demurred on his third horn of mead and remembered to wear his glasses?

And what would have occurred if Charlie Thompson, a salesman employed by Sheffield confectionary manufacturers Bassetts, had been teetotal? After an ale-fuelled party, he hopelessly mixed up his customer samples. But, quick-witted despite the drink, he passed off the sweets as a new line, launching his liquorice allsorts.

Yes, Yorkshire beer inadvertently provided work for a myriad of dentists, and it also had a hand in allowing motorists across the world to see in the dark.

One evening in 1933, Percy Shaw was drinking his favourite tipple in the Dolphin pub in Queensbury. In the age before drink/driving laws, he merrily imbibed. On his way home, he almost lost control of his vehicle, only the reflected light from the eyes of a cat at the side of the road alerting him to the presence of a deep ravine. Shaken and stirred by the experience, Percy returned to his house in Halifax and began experiments with rubber and self-cleaning glass beads and by 1934 a patent for his 'Cat's Eyes' had been secured. After the war, his invention was rolled out across Britain and by 1965 Percy Shaw had been awarded the OBE and become a multi-millionaire.

A typical immodest Tyke, Percy stayed in the simple home where he had lived with his parents from the age of two. He never married and lived a comparatively spartan life, refraining from carpeting or curtaining his living room where three television sets were permanently switched on. His greatest joy was to entertain his friends at home, regaling them with crates of beer and crisps as they watched televised wrestling. The only outward sign of his wealth was a Rolls-Royce Phantom car, which he kept in his garage. When Percy died at the age of 86 in 1976, his invention was illuminating millions of miles of road across the globe. In 2001, his 'Cat's Eyes' was voted as the greatest design of the 20th century, ahead of Concorde. Now you must agree that our Yorkshire ale is a truly gallant thing!

Yorkshire men and women have been even more effective at influencing world history when stone cold sober. One-time newspaper boy Michael

'It's 'air-raisin' stuff, Mr Faraday. Mi mop grows so fast,
I sells it ti' stuff sofas.'

PERM WAVES IN TWO DAYS!
NEW HAIR IN A WEEK!
ONLY BY USING EVANS' ELECTRIC COMB

PRICE THREE SHILLINGS. Originally 10/-

No Electric Light Required. Quite Harmless.

ALL GUARANTEED.

At last Scientific Research has achieved an effective Electric Comb at a very moderate price. Everybody knows that the root of every hair contains electricity, and the quality of this electricity determines the quality of the hair. If your hair is not wavy, crisp and springy, you can rely that it requires the gentle, stimulating electricity that only Evans' Electric Comb can give it.

REAL PERMANENT WAVES.

A natural and really permanent wave is the birthright of every woman, and Evans' Electric Comb can and does bring this desirable result in an amazingly short time. After two days you generally notice the hair forming itself into a glorious wave never to return to its former straightness, however long outstanding straight it may have been.

STOPS FALLING HAIR NOW.

Hair generally falls out because of a lack of vitality in the roots. The gentle electric current of Evans' Electric Comb flowing directly into these weakened roots, rapidly revitalizes them, and falling hair stops often in a few hours. Where there is actual BALDNESS it accomplishes marvels. New hair appears in a few days, and quite a vigorous new crop of hair has resulted after a week's use.

GREYNESS GOES FOR GOOD.

The mild soothing flow of electricity, penetrating to the minute colour glands of the scalp, makes greyness almost immediately give place to the natural colour of the hair. Dyes are useless. Evans' Electric Comb removes the cause of greyness.

Possess an Electric Comb immediately by sending the form below NOW. The remarkably cheap prices, post free, are 3/6 pocket size, 6/6 large size under plain cover. NOT ON SALE IN SHOPS.

PERMANENT WAVES IN 2 DAYS

Note the Wavy Teeth, through which comes the mild, gentle yet penetrating electricity. The battery is in the handle and will last for years. Don't hesitate. We guarantee you Beneficial Results.

MR. S. EVANS, 11, DUKE STREET, CHARING CROSS, LONDON, W.C.2.

Please send me, post free, under plain sealed cover, EVANS' ELECTRIC COMB at.................(the Large Electric Comb contains more than double the power) for which I enclose P.O. value.................

NAME................. ADDRESS.................

Faraday, whose father and grandfather came from Clapham near Ingleborough, had a 'light bulb' moment in the early 1800s after early experiments with nothing more elaborate than seven halfpenny coins, seven discs of sheet zinc and six paper sheets moistened with brine. His researches led to the creation of the electric motor and the use of electrical currents in technology and he went on to be regarded as the best experimentalist in the history of science, posterity crowning him the 'Father of Electricity.'

Another great moment in history came when, in the late 19th century, our very own Thomas Crapper left his Thorne home on foot bound for London. Now known in some circles as the 'Barnes Wallis of the Lavatory World', he introduced the royal WC, becoming plumber to the King. At great personal risk in the best traditions of Empire, he tested prototype devices on himself in his Chelsea factory, the swilling power of his creation also coping with a variety of slop substitutes – apples, sponges, cotton waste, grease, air vessels (simulating certain rubber goods whose necks were often knotted by gentlemen) and an apprentice's cap snatched from an unsuspecting head and tossed into the pan with the eureka cry: 'It works!'

Like inventors the world over, Crapper was honoured, his name becoming synonymous with a universal act performed by every living person, beast and crawling thing in the universe. So allusive, so perfect in tone and metre, so onomatopoeic, his name was God's gift to the stool, the evacuation process and anything substandard. If he had been called anything else, the world would have been a poorer place and the city of Hull would have had difficulty in finding an adjective to describe its top-town status. 'I'm just poppin' out t'netty for a Ponsonby-Smythe, darlin'', does not have the same ring to it. Does it?

Yorkshire surgeons also entered the history books in 1999, successfully concluding the first emergency operation to remove an in-growing wallet. Customers at the Red Lion in Batley dialled 999 after Charlie Clutterbust refused to buy a round. Fused to the left hip and arterial tissue, the wallet proved very difficult to dislodge, but after a ten-hour procedure it was eventually brought to the surface for the first time in many years. The wallet yielded five Roman denarii from the reign of Augustus, three groats, five gold sovereigns and a mixture of tradesmen's tokens (all in mint condition), a tightly bound wad of multi-denomination banknotes that proved impossible to unwind and a jackpot-winning national lottery ticket.

Mr Clutterbust survived the operation but was found sadly expired three days later, just like his lottery ticket. Since 1999, however, twelve similar operations have been concluded with total success, one on a woman from Bridlington. In her case, no surgery was necessary, a consultant safe breaker removing a purse from her armour-plated corset using oxy-acetylene equipment. All patients subsequently passed the Sun-Pat test. When confronted with an open carton of currants, not one of their number reached for a knife.

TEACH THISSEN TYKE

Folk Rhymes

Twelve maids went forth one morning in May,
With garlands a-singing they tripped away,
Each bearing a phial, each bearing a spoon,
Of silver as pure and as bright as the moon:
For to gather the dew on an early May morn,
Of nectar a-brimming each blossom was shorn.

(May dew was once considered to be a powerful love potion)

Castleford women must needs be fair,
Because they wash in both Calder and Aire.

The Doncaster mayor he sits in his chair,
The mills they merrily go;
His nose doth shine with drinking wine,
And the gout is in his great toe.

This tahm it's thahn,
T'next tahm it's mahn

GREAT MOMENTS IN HISTORY

An' mahn for ivver mair.

(Old charm to be repeated over a tumbling churn to ensure
a good supply of butter)

If you go to Nunkeeling, you shall find your body filling,
Of whig or of whey.
But go to Swine and come betime,
Or else you go empty away.
But the abbot of Meaux does keep a good house,
By night and oft by day.

(In reference to the monasteries in the old East Riding)

Carriages without horses shall go,
And accidents fill the world with woe:
Around the world thoughts shall fly
In the twinkling of an eye.

(Old Mother Shipton's prophesy)

York was a capital city,
When you were a nameless stew,
And therefore the heart has pity,
Dear London town for you.
You may have Piccadilly,
And flaunt Trafalgar Square,
But the lily of York was a lily,
When you were a tinker's fair!

If tha Bob dunt give ar Bob that bob that tha Bob owes ar Bob, ar Bob 'ill gie tha Bob a bob on t'nose!

CHAPTER 6

Coal, Wool, Steel and Fish

Sustained by muck and sweat, the staple industries of Yorkshire have given the county more backbone than the Pennines and a character as sharp as steel. But it was not always so.

Way before the Yorkshire pudding was invented, Brigante and Parisi tribesmen spluttered on their mammoth steaks and watched in amusement as their Roman conquerors mined lead. Then, they chuckled at the sight of Vikings struggling to dig coal from primitive bell pits. Eventually though, they warmed to the idea of work, the aborigines finally abandoning their clubs and beginning sheep farming. The iconic images of Yorkshire rams produced on the vast granges of Fountains Abbey and other monastic estates found their way into nearly every town and city crest in the shire.

Finally came the Industrial Revolution, the by now genetically absorbed hordes putting aside their hoes and ploughs and pouring into expanding settlements like Barnsley, Leeds, Middlesbrough, Sheffield and Wakefield. Here, they thrived in a frantic clamour of noise and steam – coal mines, weaving and smelt mills, giant presses, clattering, whizzing, boring, drilling and tunnelling machines of all descriptions and leviathan engines breathing grit and fire – producing fuel and goods for the world.

The workers lived, jostling for space and clean air, in serried rows of primitive hovels and back-to-back houses without sanitation or street lighting, their children, with blackened faces and their backsides hanging out, playing in the dust. But toiling 12-hour shifts, risking roof collapses, explosions, flying rocks and metal, deadly dust and fibres, scaldings, crushings, severings and limb losses all for thirty bob a week, the workers of industrialised Yorkshire never grumbled, tucking instead into their cod and chips and thanking the Lord that they had escaped the Hull trawlers.

In those days, food was scarce, siblings fighting over a crust or a scrap of fat bacon and competing with family dogs for bones. But work was everything. A man with a long stick to tap on bedroom windows and a 'wake the dead' voice preceded a mass exodus to the mines and factories, the sound of sparking clogs and the siren calls of hooters marking the start of the working day.

The hewing of coal occupied thousands and, in the early days, even young boys and girls not long out of nappies were pressed into service as water carriers and operatives of ventilation doors. Men, and some extraordinary women, worked at the coalface without proper boots, protective clothing or masks, ignoring the ever-present danger of roof falls, blinding dust, explosions and toxic gas, with absolutely no provision for de-griming at the end of the shift. But in the most appalling conditions, fun and black humour were never far from the surface.

'There were miners in their eighties down theer. We used ter tek bets on when one bloke o' eighty three would keel ower.'

'Ah've bin dead fer four years but Ah still walks round. It's too expensive to deea.'

As Lancashire with its damper climate was famous for cotton, so Yorkshire was renowned for its wool, hundreds of factories producing all manner of woven goods for export to the empire and beyond. It all began when Edmund Cartwright installed his first power loom in Doncaster in 1787. Men with big hammers tried to impede progress but by 1909, Montague Burton had

established what was to become the biggest clothing factory in the world. By 1925, his Hudson Road site in Leeds employed 10,500 people, the factory producing made-to-measure suits 'for a week's wages' and clothing one in five British men.

Like Rome, Sheffield developed around seven hills. Ready supplies of iron ore,

The blue plaque in Hudson Road, Leeds, that marks the site of Burton's clothing factory.

coal, water and brawny men with flameproof eyebrows and skin like asbestos ensured that the city would become synonymous with the manufacture of steel. The legend 'Made in Sheffield' was stamped on every quality piece of cutlery in the world and on everything else from nappy pins to naval guns. Men such as the pioneering Benjamin Huntsman, who invented the 'crucible' steel process in the 1740s, kick-started the Industrial Revolution, his city becoming Britain's arsenal during two World Wars.

Steel, wool and coal poured out of Yorkshire, nurtured by mountains of Yorkshire pudding and another iconic northern commodity. If our famous pudding is a poem in batter, then fried fish and chips is the 1812 Overture with scraps. The world's finest dish – and if it is not on the menu in heaven, I shall take my business elsewhere - is conjured in a bubbling broth of beef dripping, using only the best chipped Maris Piper and the finest fillets of haddock. No wonder St Peter put his thumbprint on the world's tastiest fish!

Most Yorkshire fish came from the port of Hull, a fleet of trawlers sailing to some of the most inhospitable, dangerous and prolific waters on the planet. Down the years, thousands of men perished in the pursuit of the ultimate supper but there was never any shortage of recruits, 'deckie learners' joining their fathers and brothers for a life of chopping ice, hauling nets and gutting. Hull produced hundreds of colourful characters, trawlermen like Walter Denton becoming legends.

Fifteen-year-old Walter started his career as a novice fisherman in 1934. A brash, forthright lad with a mischievous streak, he made a noticeable impression on his first Bonfire Night aboard. Determined to break the monotony, he secretly rigged up a bandolier of jumping crackers on deck. When the net was hauled aboard and dumped over the explosives, he waited until the mate began untying the cod end. Then he pulled the trigger, the startled and incensed mate blurting out: 'You're worse than Dillinger!', the infamous gangster at that time making bloody headlines in America.

The nickname gave the well-built Walter a certain swagger and encouraged his inclination to act the fool. He took to dressing like his namesake, sporting double-breasted suits with wide lapels and Homburg hats. He declined to carry a Tommy gun but his antics were incendiary enough.

Like Dillinger, Walter had a gang of admirers. He was so fond of these men that he had their names tattooed on his back under a colourful banner: 'My Friends'. And whenever he was in port, he would meet his pals in a pub for a 'ding-dong', numerous pints 'going down the hatch' in a smoky, guffaw-riddled atmosphere, blue with bad language. The star of the proceedings had a novel way of ordering his drinks. He would roll his banknotes into a ball and lob them at the pot man with the request: 'Get some more slurp over 'ere!'

He was always keen on making a grand entrance into his favourite den. Once he pushed open the door and rode up to the bar on a pony. Later, he bashed the door open puffing and straining on a thick mooring rope tied to a beast hidden outside. 'Come on, you beggar!' he urged with a yank of the makeshift lead. Everyone laughed when a three-week-old puppy was dragged in.

When at sea, Dillinger was partial to a tot and he devised a ruse that he tried out on several skippers. Pulling on the gear, he would emit a loud scream and pretend to have crushed his fingers, his concerned shipmates escorting him to the bridge for emergency treatment. He would refuse to take off his gloves until he had a swig of 'anaesthetic'. He adapted this trick on a later voyage, taking a coley's heart into his mouth, feigning an epileptic fit and spitting blood all the way to the rum ration.

During the Second World War, Dillinger was a volunteer seaman involved in the shipment of vital ball bearings from Sweden. He also served on armed trawlers, twice having to abandon ship. Typical of the man was an escapade involving the rescue of a gold ring from one of the doomed vessels. 'I've left my wedding ring behind!' exclaimed a shipmate looking on in anguish from a lifeboat. At these words, Dillinger slipped over the side and swam to the trawler. He returned some minutes later with the ring and another prize, explaining that the real reason for his heroics was the rescue of a bottle of grog.

Back on terra firma, the joker was always in the mood for mirth, one day acting the goat with a crèche of babies whose prams were parked outside a shop. While their mothers were inside queuing, Dillinger swapped the infants from pram to pram. When the ladies returned there was uproar and although the police were called, the perpetrator, who was sniggering nearby in an alleyway, was never brought to book.

Tragically, Dillinger died when his ship the *Kingston Turquoise* hit a reef and sank off Hoyhead in the Orkneys on 25 January 1965. He was an excellent swimmer but he drowned that day, some people say, in an attempt to save a pet dog. When his son Arthur was told the news, he is reported to have announced: 'If he's mucking about – I'll kill 'im!'

TEACH THISSEN TYKE

SAYINGS

IF EE FELL OFF T' COOP ROOF, EE'D LAND IN'T DIVI HOLE

Born lucky. The more refined and genteel Yorkshire equivalent of the southern counties' allusion to steaming equestrian excrement and the perfume of roses.

EEZ PEED ON IZ CHIPS

To jeopardise one's position, opportunities or potential. John Prescott ruined his chances of ever becoming President of the English Croquet Association after he was seen swinging his hammer like a golf club.

HEAD IN FRONT, ARSE 'ILL FOLLA

Description of rare but highly prized females common around the Skipton area, their posture and locomotion suggesting a sea-turtle/baboon hybridisation. Although lacking in femininity and charm, the so-called **HIFAWFs** are much in demand as farmers' wives; their ability to simultaneously carry heavy loads around their necks (French onion growers will pay vast premiums for the best specimens) and on specially constructed mini-howdahs on their backs making them more valuable than Landrovers.

CHAPTER 7

Country Houses

The origins of all country houses in Yorkshire derive from breeding or brass. People were either born with money, their ancestors having robbed it from somebody else in the first place, or they made it, often at other people's expense.

After the Norman Conquest, William appropriated every acre, bestowing lands as awards to the mercenaries who helped him win the fight. Nearly a millennium later, you can still detect a faint whiff of garlic and mouldy cheese over the mock battlements of certain country houses, other similar piles smelling faintly of the sweat of cotton slaves and the odour of whole generations of mine and factory workers.

What Nile navvies did for the pharaohs, cohorts of labourers and artisans did for the Yorkshire ruling classes. Similar properties in France were seized by the mob during the Terror but beyond poaching a few pheasants from their masters' woods, law-abiding Tykes muttered a bit but never resorted to violence. They preferred to wait until they made their own fortunes during the retail boom of the 1970s and 1980s and the dot.com years of the 1990s, when they could appropriate the properties for cash and set on their one-time employers as gardeners.

The archetype of the grand county house is Castle Howard, built for the Earls of Carlisle who must have had egos and bank balances the size of airships. Designed by Sir John Vanburgh, it was brilliantly described by Horace Walpole in 1772 as follows: 'Nobody had informed me that at one view I should see a Palace, a Town, a Fortified City, Temples on high places, Woods worthy of being each a metropolis of the Druids, the noblest lawn in the world fenced by half the horizon and a mausoleum that would tempt one to be buried alive; in short, I have seen gigantic palaces before, but never a sublime one.' Other mansions of similar ilk can be found at Wentworth Woodhouse, Constable Burton, Harewood, Garrowby, Bramham, York, Keighley, Nostell, Rotherham and Sheffield and in a hundred places in between.

It is amusing to reflect on the fact that at the time ordinary working people were eating wholesome, unrefined wholemeal bread in cosy cottage parlours, the gentry were having the crusts cut off their white slices, using wood and coal by the waggon load, and running from room to ridiculously large room to keep warm. But I suppose it all made work for the working man to do? And for centuries there were jobs galore as secretaries, tutors, librarians, music teachers, cooks, butlers, laundry maids, nurses, carpenters, cabinet makers (remember Thomas Chippendale from Otley?), gamekeepers and gardeners, like the talented and incomparable Lancelot 'Capability' Brown.

England's greatest gardener created 170 parks nationwide, moving tons of soil, creating scores of lakes and planting thousands of trees, many of his landscapes surviving in Yorkshire at places like Aske Hall, Hornby Castle and Sledmere. The great man refused to work in Ireland saying: 'I've not finished England yet.' A contemporary poet declared that he hoped he died before Brown, so that he could 'see heaven before it was improved.'

With some notable exceptions, all occupants of country houses tried to homogenise their households and deny their county roots. Children were forbidden to mingle with coarse urchins of the working classes, learning more about the language of ancient Rome than the vernacular of Selby market. Boys were sent to patrician schools and universities in the south of England and were immersed in the use of circumlocution, classically educated clones passing seamlessly into preordained careers as clergymen, politicians and diplomats. Girls were raised by governesses who instructed them in French, deportment and the art of the fan, the protocol of wafting away anal escapes whilst simultaneously raising the eyebrows and reproachfully staring at a servant being deemed especially important.

'Wish it did as much fer me knees.'

The matriarchs of such houses spent their days sewing Yorkshire versions of the Bayeux Tapestry, chinking china cups and conferring with cook. And the patriarchs? They spread buckshot and seed around their estates like confetti, commissioning copses, nooks and follies for the dispersal of such seed with favourite chambermaids. They spent hundreds of pounds in raising a solitary pineapple to impress their friends at the annual Christmas bash and selflessly participated in one of the biggest and longest mass experiments in medical history, hundreds of aristocrats volunteering to copulate to a state of exhaustion and to smoke, drink and feast until their faces exploded and waistcoat buttons popped, all in the interests of studying gout.

One stalwart Tyke, however, never took to indulging himself and, in the grand Yorkshire tradition, always called a spade a 'bloody shovel'. He famously cared for those less fortunate than himself, regularly entertaining the itinerant workers known as the 'Wolds Rangers' in his kitchen.

Sir Tatton Sykes was the master of Sledmere House in the East Riding. Earthy, stout, robust, unpretentious and a little prickly, he flirted with the legal and banking professions before settling for a life amongst sheep, horses and hounds. With an iron constitution and an abiding love of fitness and the outdoors, he was the keenest of walkers, travelling hundreds of miles on foot. His all-consuming passion for horses and the stud led to the creation of one of the greatest concentrations of bloodstock in the world. Succeeding to the baronetcy after the death of his brother, Tatton sold the family library of precious books and spent the entire £10,000 proceeds on more horseflesh.

*'How posh is that, mama? I can have lungs like lace curtains
and a gilded rib cage to match.'*

A punctual riser at dawn in both summer and winter, Tatton would pace the empty library every morning as part of an extensive fitness regime, recording each round circuit back and forth by placing a coin on a table. When the pile had reached a certain height consistent with the required mileage, he would repair to the buttery for breakfast. His diet, like his taste for plain, practical no-nonsense clothes, consisted of the simplest fare. Day after day, he would begin with 'new' milk followed by either an apple or a gooseberry tart laced with nuggets of mutton fat washed down with the occasional glass of port thickened with cream. After his meal, his morning was often spent riding, walking or in hard physical work either labouring in the fields or breaking up road stone. At lunchtime, he would return to Sledmere for his traditional crust of brown bread, a portion of his favourite cream cheese and a jug of home brew – the celebrated 'Old October Ale'.

An inspiration to all around him, Tatton was an expert in all forms of country crafts, excelling in hedge laying, ploughing, sowing, ditching, rick building and thatching. During his lifetime, it was said that '...there are only three things worth seeing in Yorkshire: York Minster, Fountains Abbey and Tatton Sykes'. When he died at the age of 91 another admirer commented: 'He never lost a friend or gained an enemy.'

TEACH THISSEN TYKE

VOCABULARY

Rollicking A verbal dressing down. On the advice of a friend, a long-haired Stan went to a hairdresser's shop in Drighlington and plonked down haughtily in the chair, saying: 'I get's mi 'air chopped once a year, barber, so I wants value fer money. Ah've walked ten bloody mile from Manningham 'cos me mate said yer cud do it on t'cheap like. If it's not a gud un, Ah'll give thi' such a rollickin'. Does tha bloody understand?'

'I do,' said the barber, nonchalantly snipping away. 'Who sent thee by the way?'

'Jackie bloody Pinder, that's who.'

'Oh, our mutual friend Jackie,' chuckled the barber, his electric clippers leaving a furrow an inch deep. 'I pay 'im four pund fer ivvery daft bugger he recommends.'

Snap Food. Miners' packed lunch. Sliced bread was invented in Yorkshire so that face workers could enjoy their nibbles in extremely thin seams.

Warphead A person of low intellect. 'Can ya get us a tonnip, son?' asked the farmer's wife. 'I want some veg ti go wi' t'meaat.'

'What size does tha want, mammy?' said Wilfred.

'Aboot as big as tha 'ead, lad.'

Two hours later, Wilfred returns empty handed, lamenting, 'I tried mi cap on 173 tonnips and not one were t'reet size.'

'Never mind, son,' says mammy, sighing deeply. 'Go get us some peas.'

'What size peas?'

'Aboot as big as tha brain, warpheaad!'

CHAPTER 8

Oddballs and Eccentrics

Any county that is as unique and fiercely independent as Yorkshire has its treasure of unusual people, the inclination of the Tyke to non-conformity, cussedness and disdain for authority breeding a special race of oddballs and eccentrics who blow a raspberry at status, ostentation, pomposity, fashion and convention.

We Tykes take great delight in the lampooning of folk who get too big for their designer britches, extracting the pith from dandified 'farts wi' frills on'. And, faced with brash upstarts, particularly if they have gilded plums in their mouths, we will always take a diametrically opposed line irrespective of the merits of the argument, contesting every view and supporting the underdog whatever his pedigree. What a colourful if a somewhat awkward lot we are!

Yorkshire is the biggest county in England and it has the biggest barmpots, a succession of crackpot inventors and larger-than-life characters bursting out from the history books and local folklore to tickle our ribs and test our levels of incredulity. Not for us the contrived humour of the music hall and the radio play. Why do we need such artifice when we have revolutionaries like Professor Hintelsboom in our midst?

A Wakefield lad – Joseph Aspin - invented Portland cement. After a lifetime of trial and error, Foulby clockmaker John Harrison developed the marine chronometer. Michael Faraday from Clapham near Ingleborough, as we have seen, became known as the 'Father of Electricity', and the equally prestigious title of 'Father of Aerial Navigation' was bestowed on flight pioneer Sir George Cayley from Brompton near Scarborough, the great man having his coachman pilot a glider across Brompton Dale in 1853.

Enough of the practical. What Aspin and company did for the ready mixed industry, the geriatric cruise trade, the manufacturers of vibrators and the baggage handlers at Heathrow Airport, the following gormless doylems did for mirth and gloom dispersal.

See overleaf a portrait of the famed Doctor Leica Kieper, who was called in recently by Pocklington farmer Mr Del Lewdge to investigate a resource that is set to transform the area into an international remedial and sausage-maturing centre of excellence. Therapeutic springs once brought prosperity to the Yorkshire spas of Boston Spa, Ilkley and Harrogate. Now Pocklington is set to follow suit, the exploitation of mineral waters and beneficial muds at a secret location north of the town bringing the promise of massive investment and up to 500 new jobs that are especially welcome during the current recession.

'The discovery of the spring was pure luck,' admits Mr Lewdge. 'It's been a trickle for centuries o'course. Grandfather must have buried it in a culvert at some stage and it was hidden from view until one of my largest heifers smashed through the pipe.

'The beast broke a leg in the process and was in obvious pain. Naturally, I rang for the vet to have it put down but he was delayed. And this was the amazing part. By the time he got here, the beast was running around as if nothing had happened. With it being near April last year, he thought it was a wind-up but he had an X-ray done and was gob smacked.

'The leg was caked in clart. To cut a long story short, we sent a sample to a specialist laboratory in Germany. That's when Dr Kieper from the Hydrology Institute in Baden Baden came hot foot. He had a limp like Herr Flick before he came here so he tried the mud on himself. He was so amazed! He dropped his cane and armour plated lederhosen and started running around like a greyhound with three legs. Tests have also shown that the mud can be used as a most effective coating for curing bacon and York hams, its anti-limpness properties also helping to stiffen sausages and polonies.'

'Zis mud iz also wunderbar in stiffening zer knockwurst.'

'What's next? This is wot cums from buyin' kits from Ikea.'

A Frenchman working in Yorkshire shot the first few frames in motion picture history. Louis Aime Augustine Le Prince – the 'Father of the Cinematograph' – worked from his workshop in Woodhouse Lane in Leeds, to produce amazing moving pictures of people and horses crossing Leeds Bridge in 1890. Sponsored by Dynarod and in acknowledgment of the tremendous legacy of Le Prince, MGM is currently working on a new all-Yorkshire blockbuster about the amazing life of Thomas Crapper who rid the world of foul smells and perfected the urinal and the flushing toilet. The opposite page shows a still from the work in progress taken on location in a lavatory in Hull. Starring a completely unknown Yorkshire actor whose pedigree of the latrinal world is unsurpassed, the film will be released in 2010 and will be called *Gone With the Wind.*

All Yorkshire babies are born with a congenital condition allowing them to peel oranges in their nappies. It is a chromosomal advantage of our species that inspired my father to strop blunt razor blades on his palms, putting the Gillette factory on short time, and gave me the idea for making dual use of the *Sporting Pink*, providing buttock-warming technology in our outside privy.

Gimlet-eyed Yorkshiremen are always looking for an advantage, as this wonderful old tale about a racing pig demonstrates.

In the early 1800s Coxwold landowners recruited pigs to foxhunting, their remarkable talents as pointers persuading a local farmer to begin experiments with his own sty of prize porkers. He soon discovered that they were intelligent, had noses to match anything canine, were readily taught and, surprisingly, had an electric turn of speed, albeit over short distances.

Buoyed by his success, the farmer bragged about the prowess of his pigs in a Malton inn, boasting that his animals could match any horse! Now Malton is a nationally renowned centre for horse breeding and the notion that a cloven-footed beast could beat a thoroughbred was ridiculed with a mixture of disbelief, scorn and hysterical jollity: 'I know Yorkshire ham's the best old lad ... but aren't you tekin' things a bit far?'

As the laughter receded, the company realised that the farmer was serious and an indignant racehorse owner stepped forward to put the braggart to the test. Honour was at stake. A mere breeder of swine had uttered a blasphemy and he would be made to pay for his flippancy with a wager. A race would be run for a purse of £100.

The specified two-furlong course was on level ground. The farmer was

'If he shouts "roll 'em!" one more time, I'm off!'

to be allowed to stable his contender in a sty at the starting point for one month to facilitate familiarisation with the ground and to allow adequate time for training. It was also agreed, in fairness, that the pig be relieved of a jockey and whoever rode the horse would do so in the owner's colours. For his part, the racehorse owner was permitted to select the pig, to satisfy himself that fleetness was not restricted to one exceptional animal. The pact was made and the company departed to place their bets.

A suitable pig was chosen for the race and he was dubbed *Eclipse* and transferred to his temporary sty. The training began in earnest. During the first two days of the ordeal, the pig was starved of food and persistently lashed by a man in a livery of orange and green. The third day dawned a little brighter with the offering of a bowl of swill but the blows still rained down even as the food was being poured. Ravenous and twitching in fear, poor *Eclipse* braced himself and dipped his nose in the trough. Miraculously, the beating ceased.

The ritual continued every day for the next two weeks, the pig soon realising that the tormentor only spared the rod when his victim was dining. 'Snout down snuffling!' was the maxim of the day to avoid a good hiding!

So far, so good. On the first day of the third week, the pattern of training changed. This time, the swill bucket was only shown tantalisingly to the pig for a few seconds before being carried for 50 yards up the course where it was left in full view of the salivating animal. With the whip cracking on his back, the pig cleared the ground in record time. And over the next six days, he learnt to run progressively faster to swill buckets placed ever nearer to the finishing line. By the end of the week, he was one fit pig.

The fourth week arrived and the pig realised that the worst was yet to come. He had been removed from his chums, starved, beaten, made to run like a demented rabbit and now, the ultimate horror – his arch-enemy the whip-wielding torturer, who in the past he had always managed to outpace – had been given a horse! By the end of the final week, he was even fitter still.

The day of the race arrived. The pig was rigged to a lightweight harness to prevent him bolting and he was led to the start to join the saddled horse. Piggy cogitations on yet another change of routine were abruptly ended by the appearance of a jockey dressed in orange and green. As the harness was unbuckled and the starter's flag dropped, old *Eclipse* shot away and beat the horse by several lengths, to the delight of his owner and the bookies.

'T'hoss made a reet pig's ear on it.'

Talk of pigs inevitably leads the Yorkshireman to think about pies. It is sometimes observed that the Tyke would rather have an encounter with a freshly baked pie than with a hot woman. Ask Sam Postlethwat, the gourmet featured in Chapter 2. Car manufacturers take note: to increase sales, give the pouts and the poses the elbow and modify your advertisements, draping steaming, alluring and mouth-watering pies across your boots and bonnets. Pies in Yorkshire are the stuff of legend and, as some cultures honour monolithic stone gods, we revere the pie, making the biggest monsters in the world.

Triggered, perhaps, by lunar or planetary cycles, pie mania normally strikes every 20 to 30 years. The first leviathan pie was made in Denby Dale in 1788 to commemorate the returning to sanity of King George III. The next communal madness was inspired by the Duke of Wellington's victory at Waterloo in 1815, almost a generation passing before a third pie was baked to mark the repealing of the Corn Laws. Noah's Ark had less meat than this beauty, which consumed 44½ stones of flour, 9½ pounds of lard, 16 pounds of butter, 1 calf, 100 pounds of beef, 5 sheep, 2 ducks, 2 geese, 2 guinea fowl, 4 hens, 6 pigeons, 63 small birds, 7 hares, 14 rabbits, 4 grouse, 4 pheasants, 4 partridges and 27 pear trees and other assorted timbers in its cooking. When ready, the pie was hauled by 13 horses to the dismembering ground. The 15,000-strong crowd clamoured to be served, jostling and pushing until the platform collapsed, flinging the pie to the winds, its contents being devoured without a penny being spent.

No wonder Yorkshire was ready for the next pie in 1887! Baked to celebrate Queen Victoria's Jubilee, the pie was a disaster. An excess of game was used and hot and cold ingredients were blended in a salmonellic stew, the pie moving under its own steam for an interment in quicklime.

Further pies were baked in 1928 and in 1964 but by 1988, planning for the 'Bicentenary Pie' fell foul of health and safety legislation, officials demanding that everybody involved in the production of the pie should consent to an excreta test. On the eve of the big day, inspectors arrived to carry out their final checks. They were stopped in their tracks. Simmering in a barn, the pie was guarded by a lone sentry who challenged the intruders with a cry: 'As tha 'ad thi shit tested? If tha 'asn't 'ad thy shit tested Ah've got a paper 'ere that sez tha can't cum in.' The men are reported to have left without a word.

Besides the pie, another giant confection was made in Yorkshire to commemorate the repealing of the Corn Laws, the Pudsey Plum Pudding providing an ideal theme for the next Wallace and Gromit adventure! Twenty stones of flour and basket loads of fruit were mixed in a Crawshaw Mills dye pan and the mixture was transferred to a canvas bag the size of a mainsail. Lowered back into the boiling pan, the leviathan was simmered and hauled out three days later by crane to be ceremoniously paraded through the town on a cart drawn by four white horses. Thousands of people lined the route and cheered. Afterwards, tables were erected in Crawshaw Mills yard, hundreds of diners partaking of the feast for a shilling a plate. Each portion was delicately served with a spade!

Pies and puddings apart, the most extraordinary eccentricities in Yorkshire history were displayed by a Wakefield squire. Charles Waterton of Walton Hall, near Wakefield, rode a cayman in the swamps of South America, practised regular self-purging of blood, slept with a wooden pillow under his head, greeted guests by growling and springing from concealment to bite their ankles and, on one occasion, placed his hand in a jar of venomous snakes. He also collected bird and animal specimens from his adventures, perfected the art of taxidermy, experimented in the use of the poison curare as an anaesthetic, and is credited with founding the world's first nature reserve. But if Waterton was only slightly barking, Jimmy Hirst, from Rawcliffe near Goole, was the real full-throated McCoy.

The so-called 'King of Rawcliffe' rode a bull to hounds. Never in the history of hunting have foxes been so scared, the appearance of a snorting bull and a braying madman dressed in a costume consisting of a yellow top, harlequin breeches, waistcoat, a red coat with blue sleeves and a huge lambskin hat which was three yards in circumference, made even old Reynard wave the white flag.

And Jimmy had a rapport with other beasts. He trained a pig as a pointer and, collecting other animals from the riverbank near his home for exhibition, filled his front room with multiple cages – foxes, otters, badgers, stoats and weasels squeaking and snarling alongside a bear and a monkey. He took to himself another playmate, Sarah, his assistant zookeeper becoming the most tolerant and least house-proud common law wife in history. She was responsible for dusting Jimmy's two 'pay-per-view' coffins which he kept in the kitchen. One was employed as a makeshift larder; the other had a bell fitted so that the occupant could summon his mistress from the grave!

A gregarious and friendly man, Jimmy would declare open house by giving a loud blast on his hunting horn. A compulsive gambler, he often fell foul of

the bookmakers. Short of cash but undeterred, he issued his own banknotes with the following inscription: 'At the River Bank of Rawcliffe, I Promised to Say Five Farthings.' Incredibly, he sold thousands of the notes, surviving specimens fetching large sums at auction.

Jimmy became so famous that he was invited by King George III for tea. Before the big day, attendants sought to prepare the Yorkshireman for the formalities of a royal visit. 'Damn your forms and ceremonies,' sparked Jimmy. 'If the king don't like my ways he must let it alone. I didn't seek his acquaintance – he must take me as I am. I'm a plain Yorkshireman.' He

'Ah wants eight virgins ti carry mi coffin.'
'None aboot, Jimmy. I've tried six convents already.'

described His Majesty to his face as 'a plain old chap', the king noting that his guest exhibited the archetypal 'Yorkshire Bite'.

But Jimmy left the best until last. He died at the age of 91 in 1829, and insisted, in his will, that he be carried to the grave by eight old maids. But geriatric Amazons were rather thin on the ground in 1829 and Jimmy had been fond of a calorie or two. And even if eight muscular grandmas had been found, how would they have qualified for the job, bearing in mind the will's further stipulation? The pallbearers were, you see, each to swear on oath to a state of virginity. Never one for spending silly money, Jimmy promised each of the virgins half a guinea. The money was never paid.

To finish, I give you one bonehead who could qualify as the 'Lame Under T'Cap Supreme Champion' and a skinflint who continues to give Yorkshire a bad name.

Lumley Kettlewell, the son of a farmer and merchant from Bolton Percy, believed it was possible to live without food, theorising that eating was merely an acquired habit. Quitting his shop in York, Lumley began testing his hypothesis on his prize horse, lamenting: 'As soon as the beast grew accustomed to living without food, it died.' Undeterred, he began experimenting on himself, his only sustenance coming from the begging bowl or from the gutter. He lived in a large wooden crate, entering his abode by way of a ladder leading to an upper window. Remarkably, he lived to the ripe old age of 68, dying in 1819.

Old John Mealy-Face who was born in Topcliffe in 1784 has the reputation of being the meanest man in Yorkshire history. And (in a whisper) that is some achievement! During his frequent absences from home, he refused to allow his hungry wife to bake bread. On one occasion, she disobeyed her husband, taking flour from the bin without permission. Not being prepared to waste money on a lock, he conceived an infallible strategy to counter the theft, impressing his large head into the top of the flour before leaving the house and repeating the operation on his return to ensure that not a dusting had been removed.

TEACH THISSEN TYKE

VOCABULARY

Fettle To clean or to put into good working order. A good housewife will fettle her doorknocker so often that it disappears. However, over-enthusiasm in the scrubbing of shirt collars and underpants needs to be curbed to prevent fabric and brush disintegration. Vigour may be tempered by applying the **zulloil** procedures outlined in Chapter 1 and by substituting dry meal for beef in the diet. To counter garrulousness and dissolute ways, pregnancy should be aspired to as the optimum condition for any Yorkshire woman of breeding age, the synonymous terms 'She's in fine fettle' or 'I'd like to fettle yon' alluding to both the actuality and the intent.

Fratching Arguing. Verbal, high decibel fencing over the garden wall usually between identically dressed women. Floral pattern marquee-type dresses, stained aprons, knotted headscarves and carpet slippers are the preferred fratching ensembles of all Yorkshire women although there are regional variations in the choice of gesticulation sticks. West Riding exponents prefer besom brushes; North Riding ladies choose mops. The archetype of the genre is Nora Batty, the star of the popular TV show *Last of the Summer Wine*.

Fratchers, like their very stable companions the **HIFAWFs** (see Chapter 6) are in great spousal demand, their ability to ward off intruders and debt collectors obviating the need for the employment of pit bulls and the installation of CCTV and alarm systems.

SALUTARY WARNING ON LEAVING

'If yer finds yersen up t'spout, stop thrustin'.'